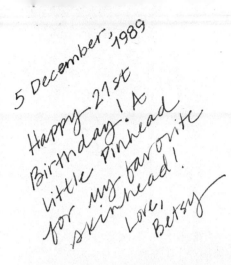

5 December, 1989

Happy 21st
Birthday! A
little Pinhead
for my favorite
skinhead!
Love,
Betsy

ZIP-PIK Artists: (left to right, in order of appearance)

FRONT

Jonathan Rollins	Paul Swartz
G. Johnson	Sam Wilschke
Leslie Brokaw	Joe Zabel
Francisa Lohmann	Ben Stone
John V. Cody	Bob Polaski
Jim Lucio	Benjamin Smith
Cathy Nordling	Lisa M. Brown
F.A. Powers	Doug Bertrand
Stephen Hartwell	Carrie Schneider
Elby Buttery	Mikey Morrison
Tom Acquario	Jeremy Whitt
Scott Thomas	Thea Guenther
S. McClusky	Denny Holland
Rob Burg	Dave Dugan
Luke Atkinson	Ray Waters III
Larry Chin	Jim McMahan
Robin Van Marth Wilson	Val Akula
D.B.	Kurt Larsen

BACK

Phil La Force	Steven Mulvey
Wyman Choy	Sheryl Fitzmaurice
T. Driscoll	John Urbanowski
Trent Thornton	Jeff Ecker
Keith Webster	Gregory Eddy
Maribeth Lemay	Dave Manley
Reed Sturtevant	Terry King
Joe Hankin	Kristin
James V. Lee	Charlie Hultgren
John Armiger	Wendy Dunning
Cathy Nordling	Braden Pastore
Laura Mooney	Jon Buller
Bob Lezon	Cady Ann Goldfield
Danielle Wonder	Marc Crisafulli
Joel Boucher	Dave Knepper
Jeff Song	Edwin Newman
Glen Enloe	Mitchell McConnell
Gene Mendez	Toby Morton

PINHEAD'S

PROGRESS

E. P. DUTTON • NEW YORK

Published in the United States by E.P. Dutton, a division of NAL Penguin Inc.,
2 Park Avenue, New York, N.Y. 10016.

Published simultaneously in Canada by Fitzhenry and Whiteside, Limited, Toronto.

Library of Congress Catalog Card Number: 88-51455

ISBN: 0-525-48468-X
Book design and production: Bill Griffith
Typography: Ampersand Design
Camera Work: G. Howard, Inc.

10 9 8 7 6 5 4 3 2 1

First Edition

"Can we realize for an instant what a cross-section of all existence at a definite point of time would be? While I talk and the flies buzz, a seagull catches a fish at the mouth of the Amazon, a tree falls in the Adirondack wilderness, a man sneezes in Germany, a horse dies in Tartary and twins are born in France."
William James
The Principles of Psychology, 1890

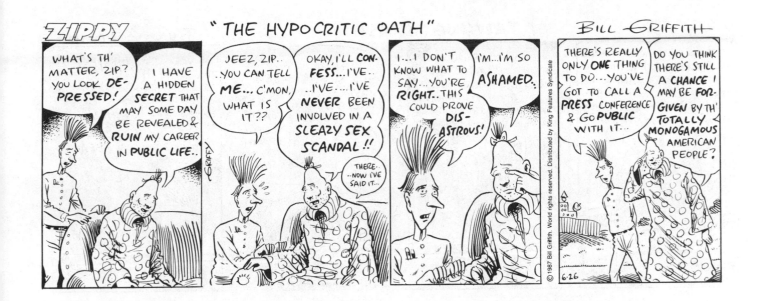

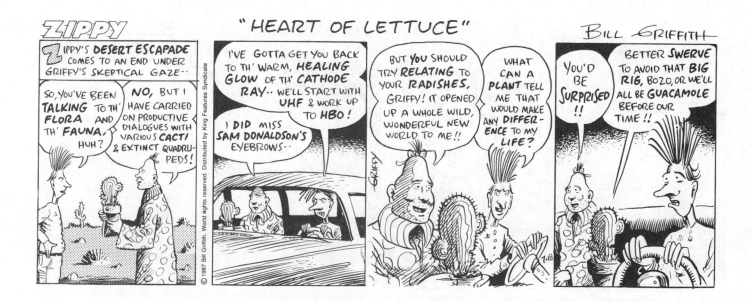

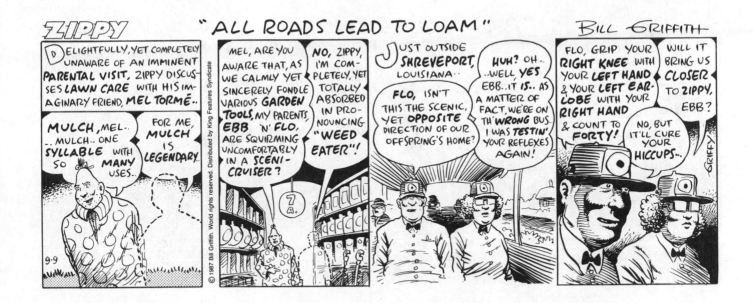

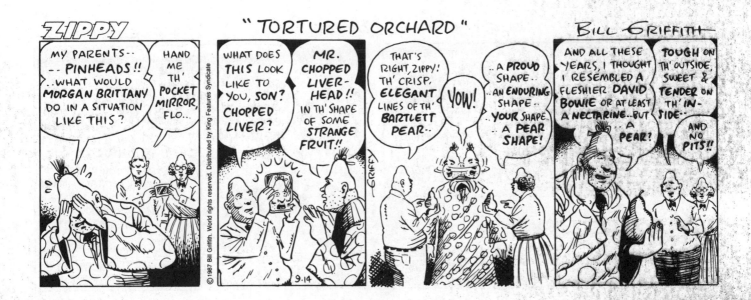

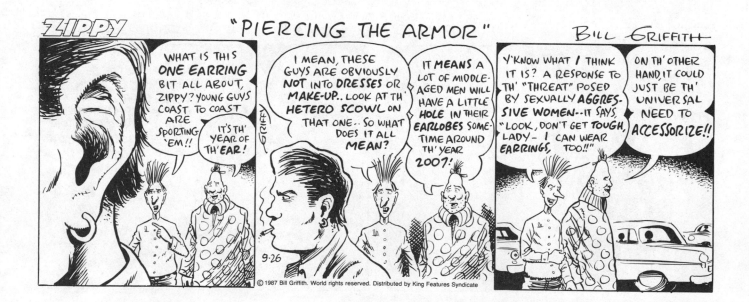

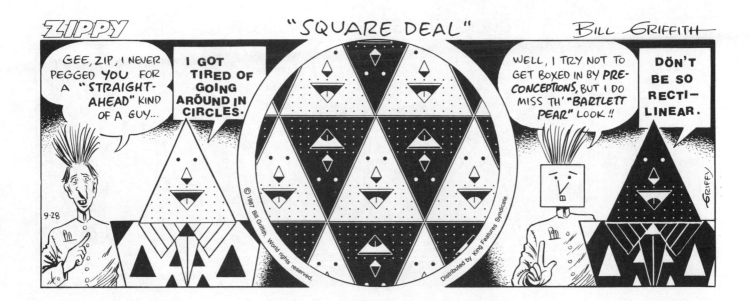

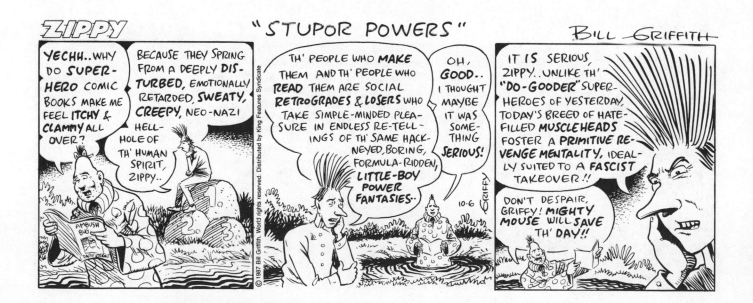

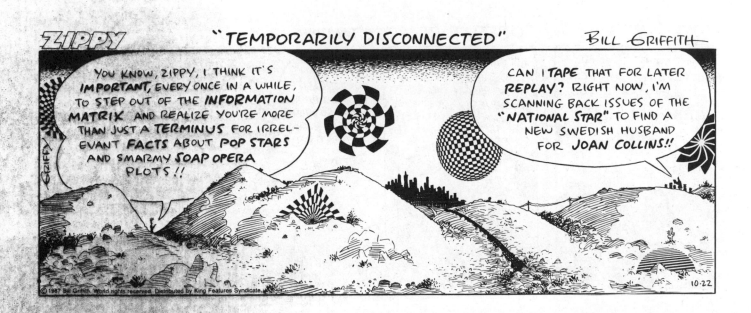

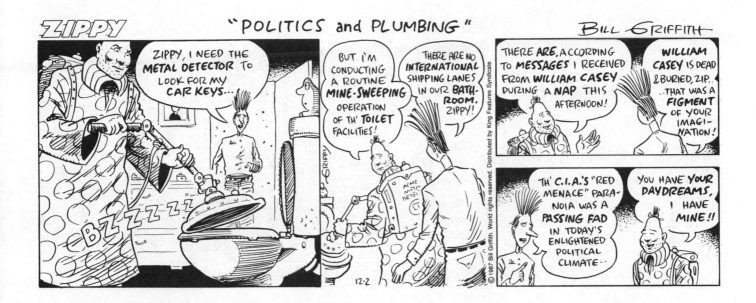

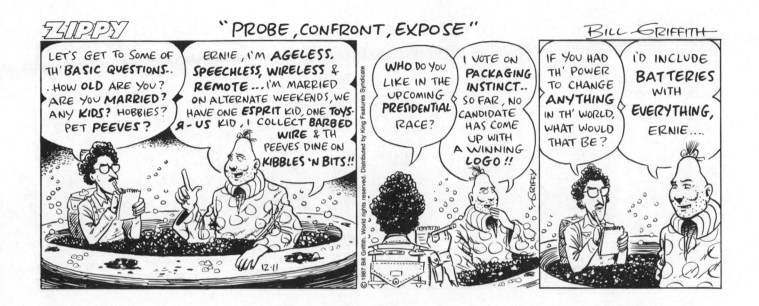

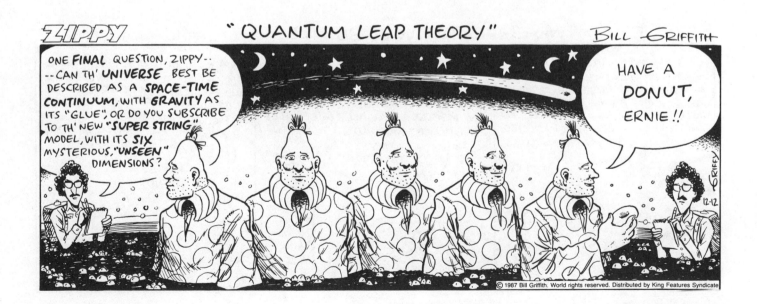

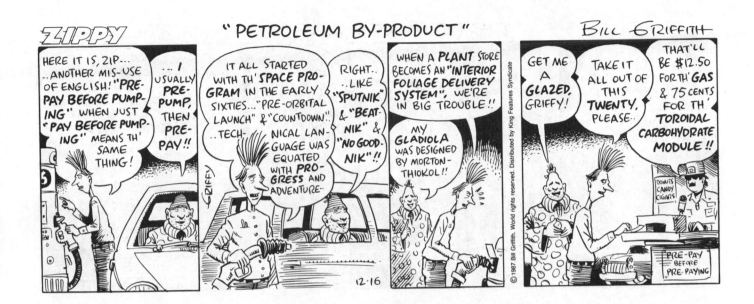

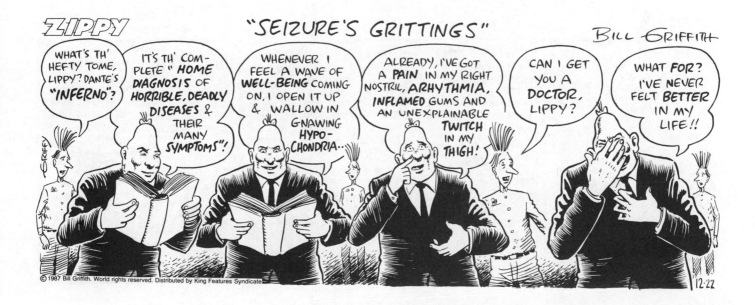

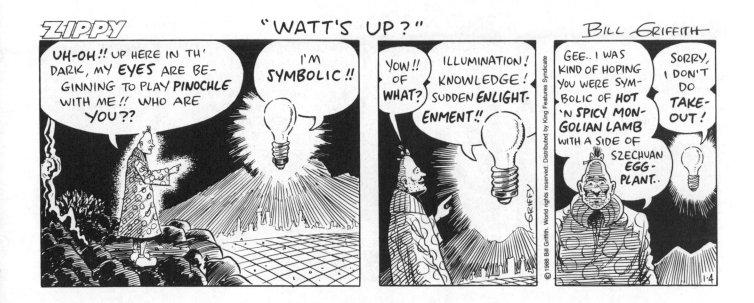

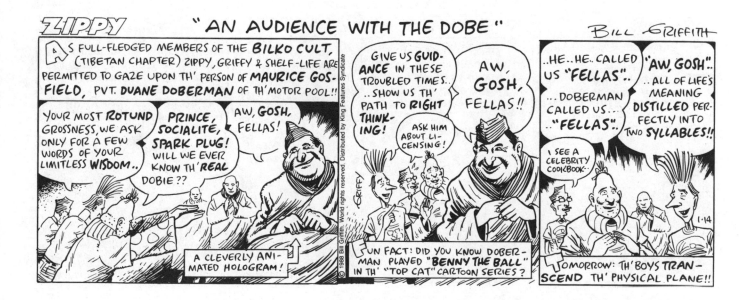

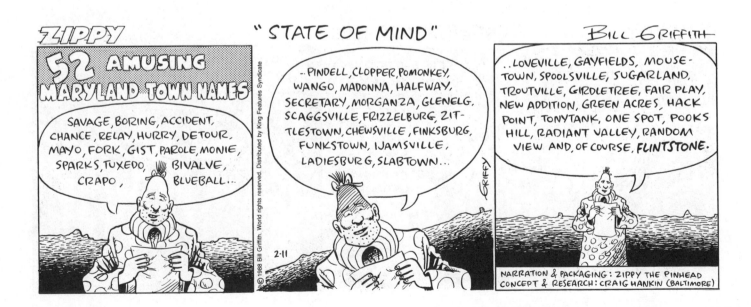

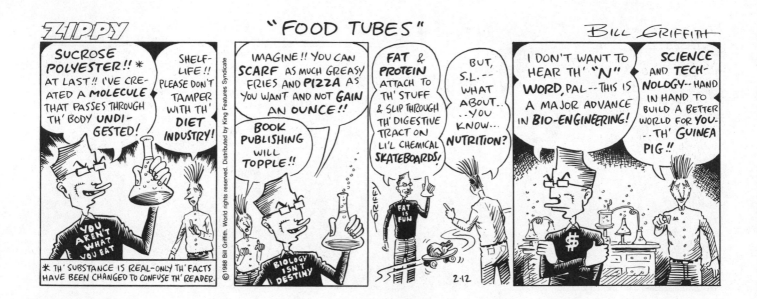

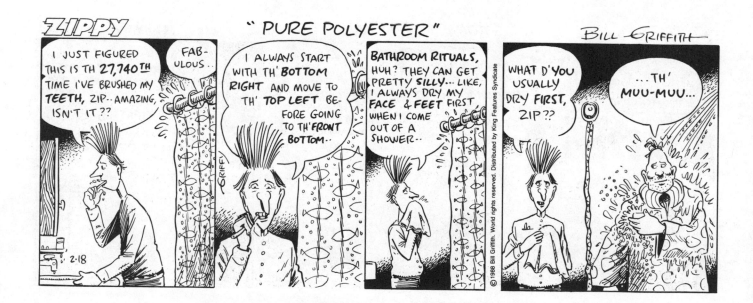

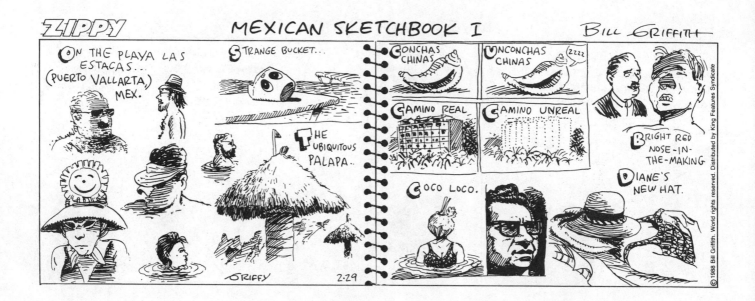

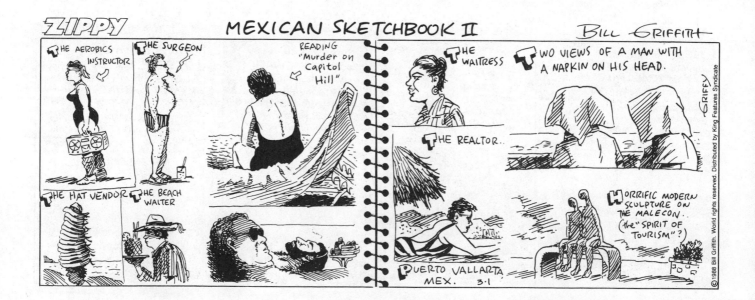

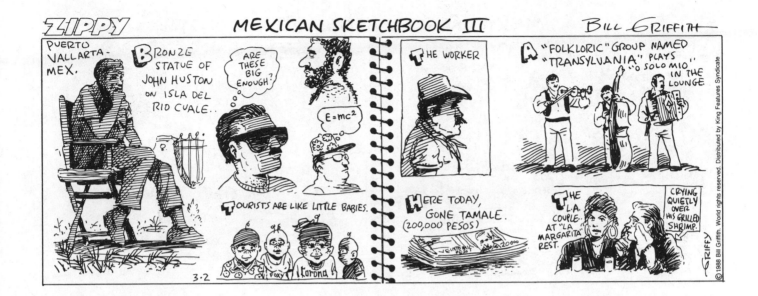

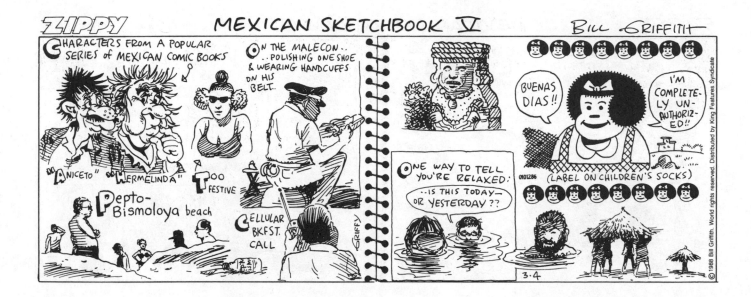

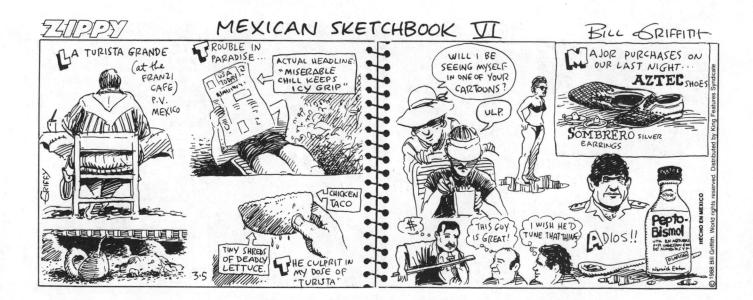

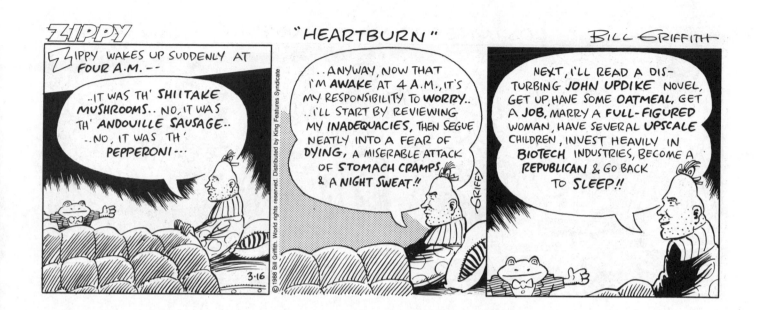

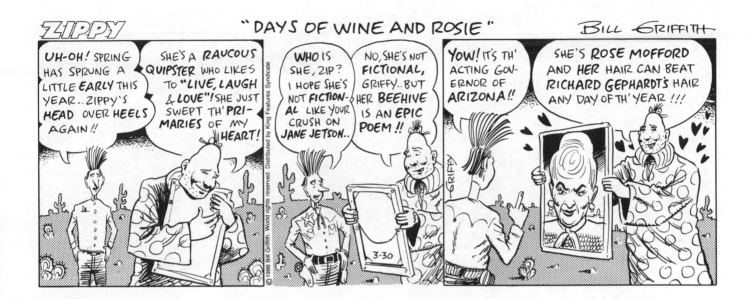

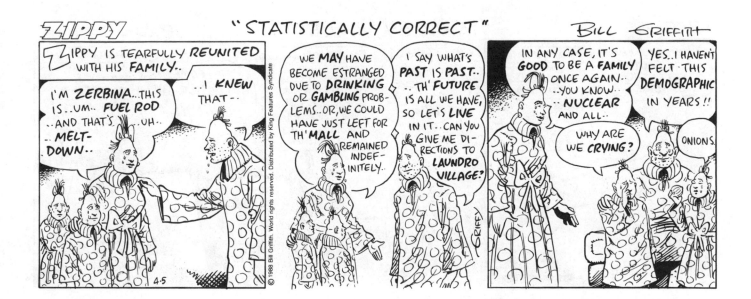

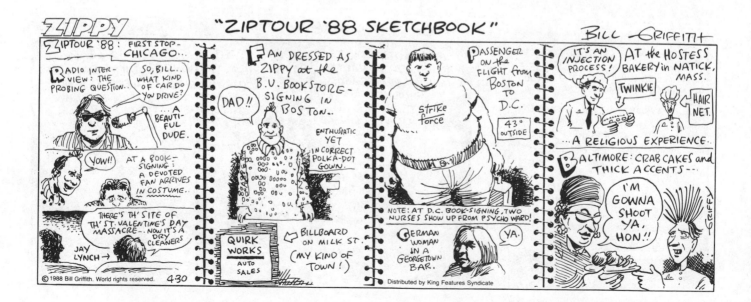

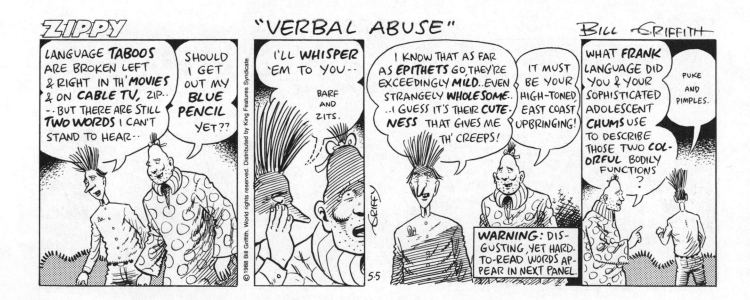

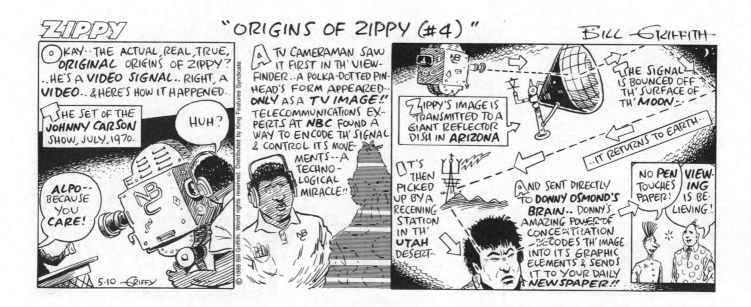

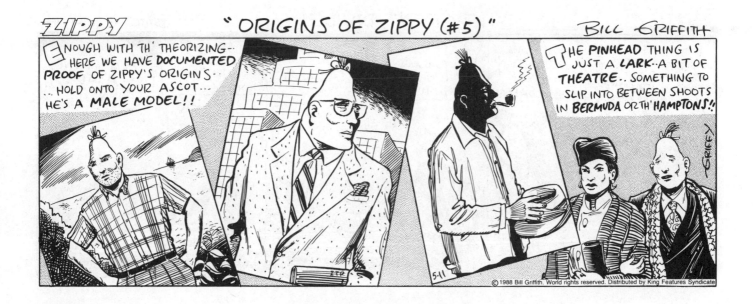

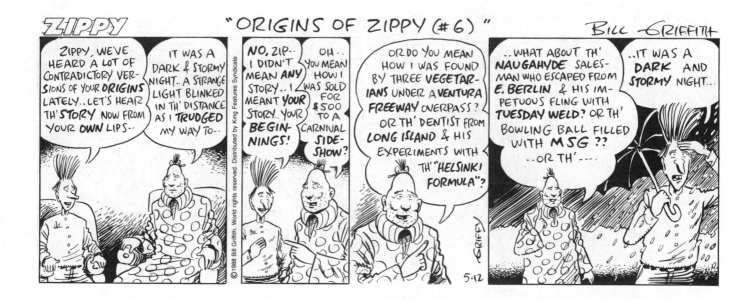

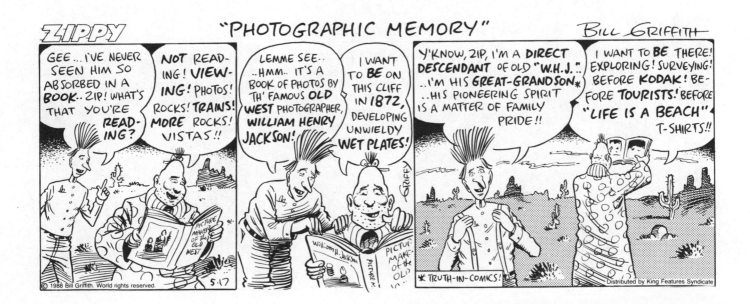

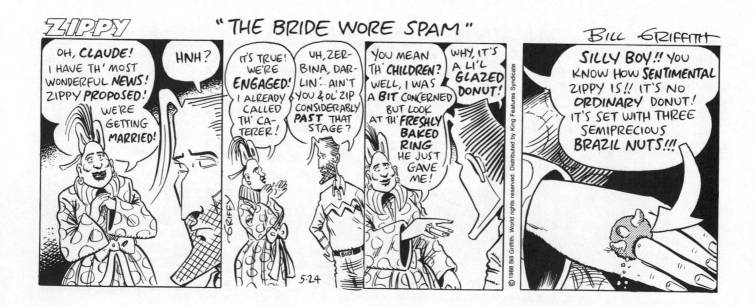

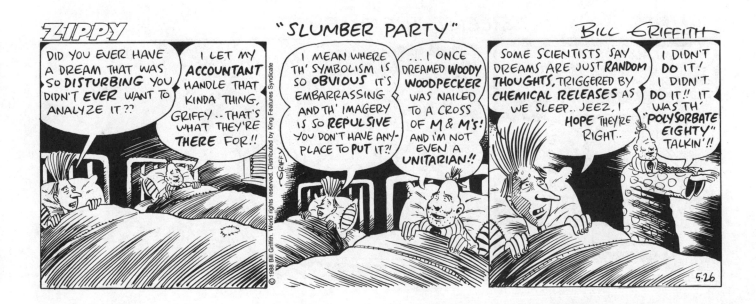

ZIPPY

BILL GRIFFITH

THERE ARE FACES AND, THEN, THERE ARE **FACES**--

SOME FACES ARE **MASKS**.. OTHERS ARE LIKE **ARCHITECTURE**..

LET'S **FACE IT**! WE HAVE OUR **FAVORITES**!!

JACK PALANCE..NOW **THERE'S** A **FACE**.. A FACE LIKE THE SIDE OF A **CLIFF**... A FACE WITH **GEOGRAPHY**..

6.1

KEEP ON **SMILIN'**, JACK!!

ZIPPY

"ABOUT FACE (#2)"

BILL GRIFFITH

YOU KNOW WHO HAS AN **INCREDIBLE FACE**, ZIP? A FACE LIKE A **JAPANESE MASK**? A BEAUTIFUL JAPANESE MASK?

BANG, ZOOM, GRIFFY! YOU MUST BE REFERING TO **AUDREY MEADOWS**, TH' BELOVED "**ALICE KRAMDEN**"!

HER **HAUGHTY EXPRESSION** STIRRED MANY A **STRANGE DESIRE** IN ME AS A **BOY**, I MUST CONFESS..

SIGH..

SIGH..

WHAT ABOUT HER **CRISPLY STARCHED**, '50s "**UNIFORM**" **DRESSES**? AND THAT CUTE **HALF-APRON**?

OF COURSE, WE ALL KNOW WHERE **WILMA FLINTSTONE** CAME FROM!

TAKE ME TO **BED-ROCK**!

6.2

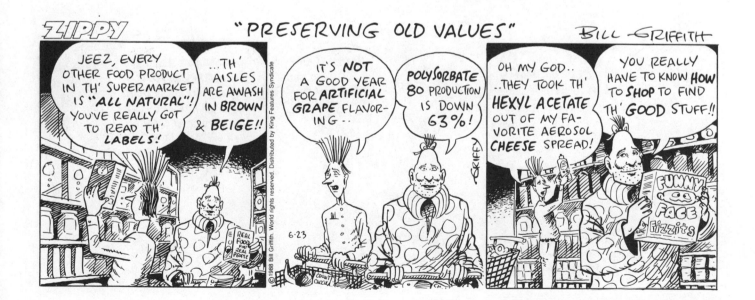

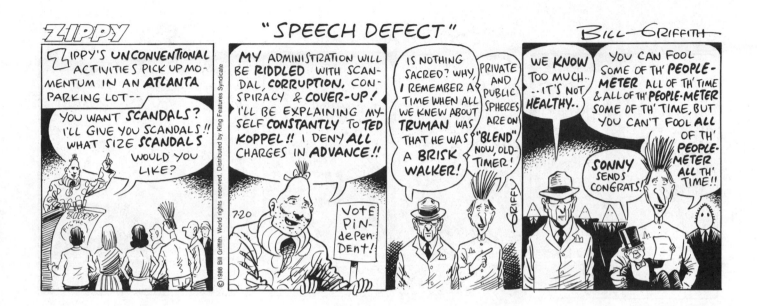

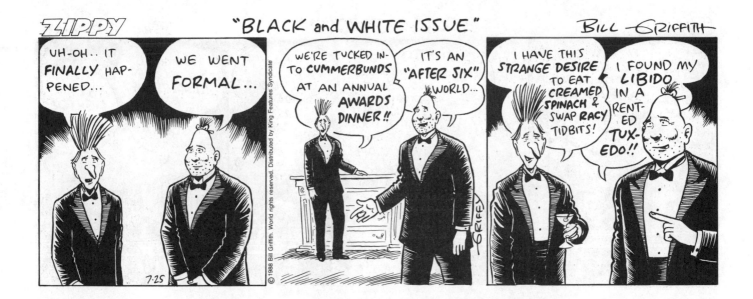

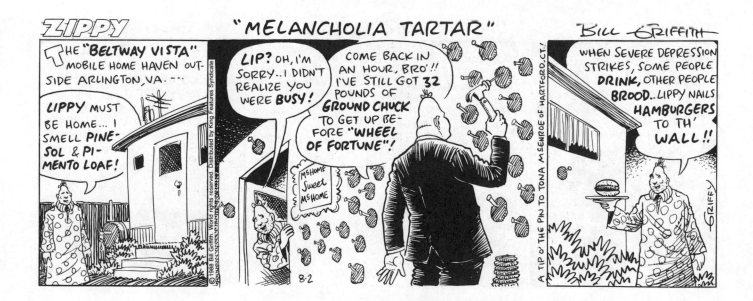

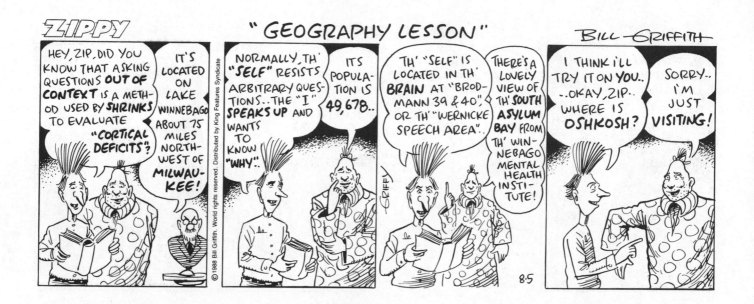

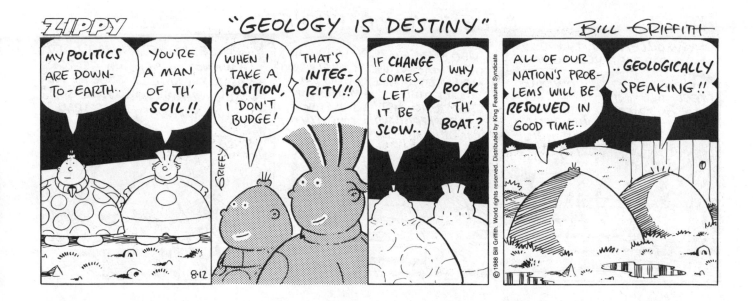

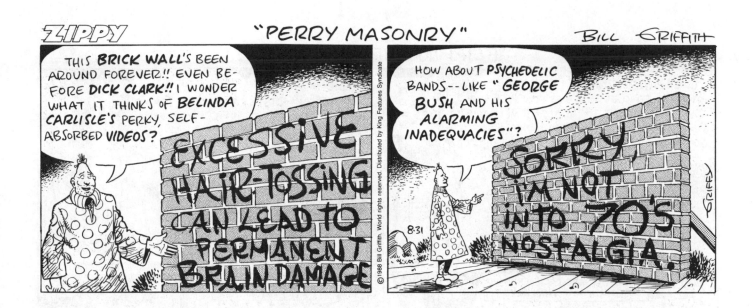

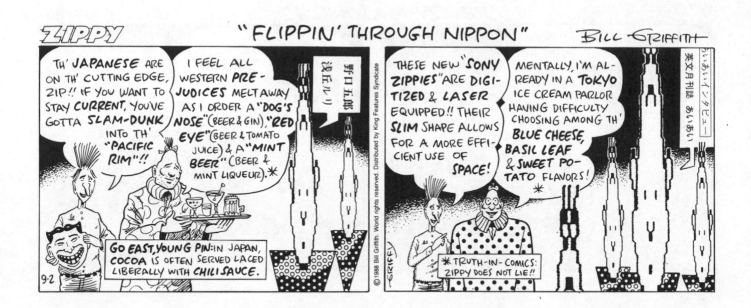

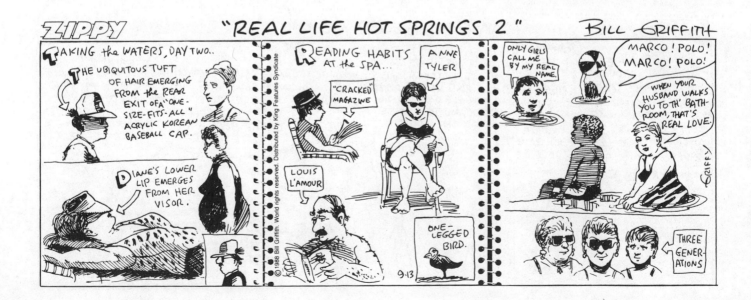

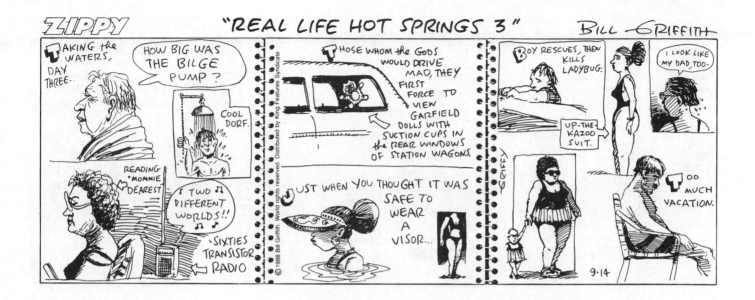

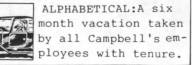

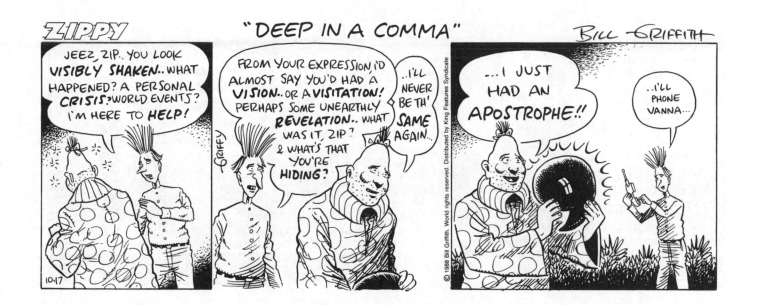

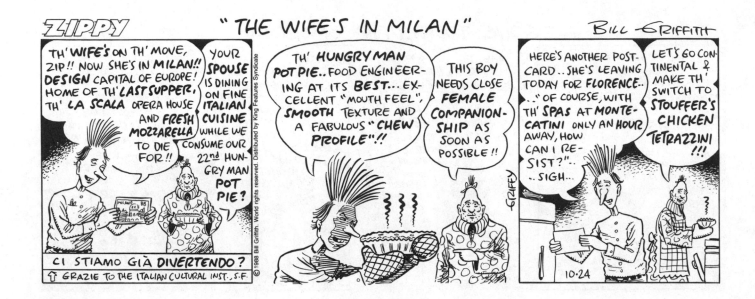

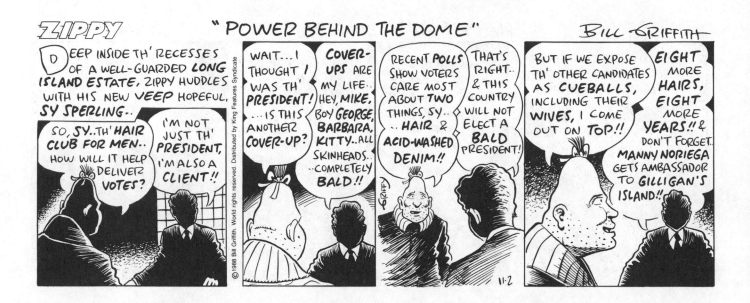

ZIPPY — "MICRO-MINUTE" — BILL GRIFFITH

Panel 1: ONE DAY, ZIPPY HAD A **VERY IMPORTANT** REVELATION...

EVERYTHING I CAN **TASTE, TOUCH** OR **SMELL** IS PART OF **TASTING, TOUCHING** OR **SMELLING!**

Panel 2: THE NEXT SECOND, HE HAD **ANOTHER** VERY IMPORTANT REVELATION...

EVERYTHING I CAN **SEE** OR **HEAR** IS PART OF **TELEVISION!**

Panel 3: SUDDENLY, HE HEARD A VOICE FROM ABOVE.. KIND OF LIKE **RAYMOND BURR**..

ZIPPY!! THIS IS **GOD**!! YOU HAVE TO COME TO YOUR **SENSES** & **CHOOSE** WHAT'S **REAL**!!

11·14

Panel 4: **TASTING, TOUCHING** AND **SMELLING** ARE VASTLY OVERRATED!!

ZIPPY — "BLOW IT UP REAL GOOD" — BILL GRIFFITH

Panel 1: **ACTION** IS **EVERYTHING** THESE DAYS...

POW.

Panel 2: ..FILM, TELEVISION, EVEN POPULAR FICTION.. ..IT HAS TO **MOVE**.. CAR CHASES, EXPLOSIONS, DARING RESCUE ATTEMPTS...

SMASH.

Panel 3: THE NEW **"KIDULT"** AUDIENCE DEMANDS CONSTANT STIMULATION.. ..**CONTEMPLATION** IS A DIRTY WORD.. IN FACT, **"WORDS"** IS A DIRTY WORD.. ENTERTAINMENT MUST BE **FELT IMMEDIATELY** TO SUSTAIN VIEWER INTEREST..

SPLAT.

11-15

Panel 4: ..QUICK SIGHT GAGS, LOTS OF VIOLENCE, SEX AND EXPLOSIONS.. **LOTS** & **LOTS** OF **EXPLOSIONS** -- THESE ARE THE IMPORTANT THINGS.. PLOT, MOTIVATION, CHARACTER.. ..THEY JUST GET IN TH' WAY.. ..WRITING, DIALOGUE, REPARTEE .. THESE MUST BE AVOIDED AT ALL COSTS.. ACTION, ACTION IS WHAT THEY WANT.. ..ACTION, ACTION AND MORE **ACTION** !!!

KA-BLOOEY.

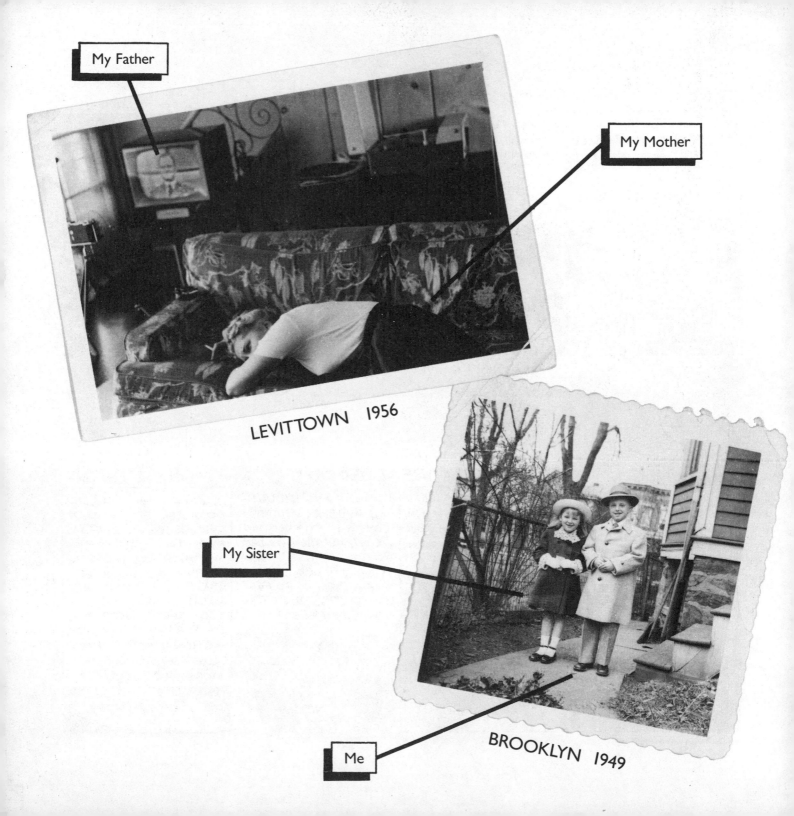

My Father

My Mother

LEVITTOWN 1956

My Sister

Me

BROOKLYN 1949